Do Right
YOUTH

TABLE OF CONTENTS

DAY 1:

WHAT IS SIN?

Do right. Obey.

You probably hear those words a lot. Your parents and teachers all want you to do the right thing. They want you to make your bed, do your school work, and put your clothes in the laundry basket. Have you ever wondered why they ask you to do these things?

I'm sure you have. And although you can tell yourself it's because they are mean, I'm sure you know it's because they love you and they want what's best for you. So, now I need to ask you a big question. Do you do the right thing? Take a minute and think about that, then be honest with yourself.

If you were honest, your answer was no. We don't always do the right thing. Why? Well, we will talk about that a lot in this study. But first, let's understand a few basics. Read Romans 3:23. Write it below.

_____

The Bible makes it clear that we have ALL sinned. Before we can figure out what to do about this problem, we need to take a look at what SIN really is.

I know you've heard the word "sin" before, but do you know what it means? Write anything that comes to mind below. We will compare your thoughts to what you learn through this study at the very end.

SIN IS_____

_____

_____

Look up the word SIN in a Bible dictionary. In your own words, write a definition for sin below.

SIN IS_____

_____

_____

Look up the following verses and tell how they describe sin.

1 JOHN 3:4	DEUTERONOMY 9:7

For this study we are going to look at sin in two ways:
1. Doing what is WRONG in God's eyes.
2. NOT DOING what is right in God's eyes.

The Bible has so much to say about how we sin. Let's look at Philippians 4:6-9 to see the three main areas where we are most likely to have trouble. After each reference record some specific instructions God has given us.

Philippians 4:6-7 tells us how to pray.

_____

_____

Verse 8 tells us how to think.

_____

_____

And verse 9 tells us how we should live.

_____

_____

End today by writing or drawing a prayer to God in response to all you have learned about sin today.

_____

_____

_____

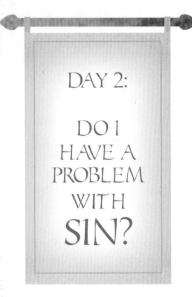

DAY 2:

DO I HAVE A PROBLEM WITH SIN?

Yesterday we read in Romans 3:23 that we have all sinned against God. But most Christians have a hard time believing this. We try to do good things, help people, and we say our prayers at night. Since we haven't murdered anyone or stolen anything, sometimes we think we haven't really sinned.

This couldn't be further from the truth. Let's read a few more verses about sin and see what we can learn. After you read the verse, write what you learn about sin.

ISAIAH 53:6

_____

_____

_____

1 JOHN 1:8

_____

_____

PSALM 14:3

_____

_____

ISAIAH 64:6

_____

_____

The interesting thing about sin is that it's different for each person. The things I struggle with are probably not the same exact things you struggle with. It's not different because the Bible changes. It's different because we are different from each other. Let's read James 1:14. What does it say we are tempted by?

_____

Now go back and circle the word that describes WHOSE desires are the problem. The Bible says we are only tempted by the things we desire. That means we might not be tempted by the same things as our friends or our siblings. It also means we need to be very careful about what we desire because these are the things that will often trap us into sin.

Let's read James 1:15 and see what happens when we give in to the things we desire (or the things we WANT)! This verse shares 3 things that happen. Draw the step-by-step process below. In the first box, draw one specific desire or want that you have, then show what happens to it.

FIRST	NEXT	LAST

It's pretty clear. Sin causes death. We see that in James and in Romans 6:23. What other problem do we see in Isaiah 59:2?

_____

_____

So what are your sins? Remember I said they are probably different for you than they are for your friends or siblings. Let's make a chart to help us see where we have the most difficulty. Remember to be honest. God already knows and you can't fix this if you aren't willing to tell yourself the truth.

In the chart below write some of the things you desire on the left side. These things don't have to be "bad" things. Anything we want more than we want to obey God can lead us to making poor choices. On the right side of the chart, write or draw something sinful you might do (or have already done) because of your desire. For example, my desire might be a chocolate chip cookie and I might steal to get it or say ugly words to a sibling in an effort to keep them from getting the bigger one.

DESIRES	SIN THEY MIGHT LEAD TO

If you need help thinking of sins, these passages might help: Exodus 20, Galatians 5:19-21, and Ephesians 5:3-6.

We are going to stop here today, but if you are feeling guilty about all of this sin, I want you to know that I'm going to share some really good news with you tomorrow. For now, pray and ask God to teach you what He wants you to learn.

DAY 3:

JESUS DIED FOR THAT

After yesterday you might be feeling pretty guilty and hopeless about sin. At least you should feel that way when you are faced with the truth of your own sin. We will never get this right on our own. It's impossible. So impossible that the very first people to ever live only had one single rule to follow and they still couldn't do it. Take a few minutes and read Genesis 3, then tell the story in your own words below.

_____

_____

_____

_____

_____

_____

_____

I don't know about you, but that sure seems hopeless to me! Adam and Eve got to walk and talk with God every day and yet they still couldn't please Him. Since you and I don't have that, do we have any hope at all? What do you think?

_____

_____

Let's read Romans 5:8-10 and see what the Bible says. After you read, answer the questions below.

Who did Jesus die for?_____

Were you still a sinner when he died for you? _____

He died to save you from what? _____

It's all good news! We absolutely have hope even when we are guilty of sin. In fact, we have nothing but hope! God sent His only Son to cover our sins. But there is one catch to this. Do you know what that is?

_____

Please read John 3:16 and write what it means below.

_____

_____

_____

The Bible promises that God washed all of our sins away through the death of His Son, Jesus. If we believe in Him, we can ask for forgiveness and be free from our sins forever. If this is something you've never done before today, please talk to you parents or your pastor about it before you go any further in this study.

If you've already done that, have a parent help you write your testimony in the space below. Add some pictures too if you'd like. This is one of the most wonderful stories of your life!

_____

_____   _____
_____
_____
_____
_____
_____
_____
_____

_____
_____
_____
_____
_____

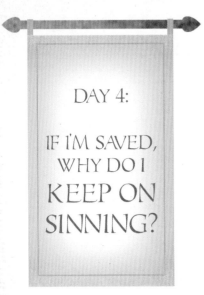

DAY 4:

IF I'M SAVED, WHY DO I KEEP ON SINNING?

Yesterday we talked about how we are saved from the penalty of sin and how God forgives us of those sins through the death of His son Jesus. You might be wondering what a lot of people wonder. If Jesus really saved me from my sins, why do I keep on sinning?

That's such a hard question to understand. We are going to talk about it a lot over the next few weeks, but the first thing you need to understand is exactly what the cross does for our lives.

Let's read Romans 6:23. What is the penalty for sin and what does Jesus offer instead?

_____

_____

_____

_____

Through Jesus' death, we are free from the ultimate PENALTY of our sin. We will not face an eternity in hell. The ultimate price of death has already been paid. This doesn't mean we won't have consequences for our sins. In fact, we almost always will. Those consequences will be one reason to stay away from sin as we will see next week.

Now let's read Romans 6:14 and 6:22. What do these verses promise us?

_____

_____

_____

Here we see that we are free from sin's POWER over our lives. We can say no to the temptation because of what Jesus did for us. We don't have to be slaves anymore, just doing whatever our desires tell us to do. We will learn a lot more about this, but first let's read Galatians 1:4 to see the final thing we are free from.

_____

_____

_____

Isn't that great news? One day we will be free from the PRESENCE of sin. We will live in heaven where there will be absolutely no sin around us. And we will never sin again. I can hardly wait for that day. Can you?

As we end our study today, journal your thoughts below. Think about what you have learned about sin. Pray and ask God to help you learn more and be willing and ready to use these truths in your life.

DAY 5: THE NEW LIFE

Have you ever thought about your responsibilities as a Christian? Once we become free from our sins by believing in Jesus and asking for forgiveness, we have responsibilities. The Bible says we cannot keep living a life just like those who don't believe in Jesus. We must live a new life. Let's read Ephesians 4:17-24 to see what we are called to do in this new life.

How do the Gentiles (unsaved) live according to verses 17-19?

_____

_____

_____

How are we supposed to live according to verses 20-24?

_____

_____

_____

If we believe God and want to follow Him, the Bible says we are born again. We get a new life, not like a baby gets a new life though. We get this new life through the renewing of our minds. This means we get it by reading the Bible and learning more about God. As we do that, our new self becomes more and more like God.

Now read verses 25-32 and write some of the keywords for how we should live in the box below.

> **HOW WE SHOULD LIVE**
>
>
>
>
>
>
>
>

Do you think it's easy to do this? I sure don't! We have to keep trying to live our lives like Jesus, but it's not easy at all. We are going to fail many times. We are going to face great temptation, too. Satan, the world, and our own flesh works very hard to trick us into sinning. We've got to be ready. Next week, we are going to learn exactly how to do that, but first let's read Micah 6:8 and see what God calls us to do.

Does that verse say you need to be perfect? _____

What keywords does it use?

_____

_____

As you finish the study this week, pray and ask God to help you know Him more so you can live this new life and walk humbly with Him.

_____

_____

_____

_____

_____

_____

_____

_____

_____

_____

_____

_____

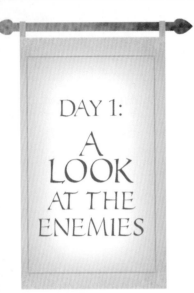

DAY 1: A LOOK AT THE ENEMIES

Last week we talked about how we are all guilty of sin. We also learned that as Christians, we are free from the power of sin and ready to obey God as a new creation. However, as we saw on Day 4 last week, while we are still on earth we will never be free from the presence of sin. In fact, we have three main enemies always trying to keep us from obeying God and walking upright. This week we are going to learn about these three enemies and find some ways to fight them.

ENEMY #1: THE WORLD

One person who was attacked often by the world was Daniel. Read Daniel 1:1-7 and create a small timeline of Daniel's life in the box below.

In the book of Daniel we learn about three ways the people of Babylon tried to tempt Daniel and his friends to do something against God. Let's read each one and record what happened.

DANIEL 1:8-21

_____

_____

_____

DANIEL 3:4-29

_____

_____

_____

DANIEL 6:4-22

_____

_____

_____

In all three of these examples the people of Babylon wanted Daniel and his friends to be like them. They didn't like the way they acted or their worship of God. But what did Daniel always do?

_____

What did Jesus tell us about the world in Matthew 10:22?

_____

_____

What specific ways does 1 John 2:15-17 instruct us in how to resist the world?

_____

_____

_____

_____

Daniel lived many years before those words were written, but he clearly knew the truth found in them and was able to stay away from the desires of the world. How are you doing with that? Write a prayer below asking God to help you.

_____

_____

_____

_____

_____

_____

_____

_____

DAY 2: THE FLESH

Yesterday we talked about how the world tries to talk us into sinning against God. You might not be old enough to have been tempted by other people, but you are definitely tempted by your own flesh every single day. Did you know that?

Let's read James 1:14. What does the Bible say we are tempted by?

_____

_____

Now read verse 15. What happens when we give in to our own desires? Write it out on the line.

_____

Let's read about a man who gave in to his desire. Who are the two people in Genesis 25:29-34?

_____ AND _____

Read Genesis 25:29-34 and write/draw about what happens.

WHAT IS A BIRTHRIGHT?

A **birthright** was a very important thing in Bible times. It was a privilege given to first-born sons honoring them with special rights, a larger inheritance, and authority over the father's money and property as he got older. Esau sold his birthright for what? _____

Can you believe he sold it for a bowl of stew? This was a serious case of giving in to his fleshly desires. That would be like you giving away your house and all of your belongings just to have a fresh-baked cookie.

Seems crazy, but this is the way our desires work. We are easily tempted by the things we want to have and can sometimes do crazy things to get what we want. Can you think of a time when you did something crazy to get what you wanted?

_____

_____

_____

Let's read Galatians 5:17. Draw a picture of what the verse is telling us.

Now read the last part of the verse again. Because our flesh is against the Spirit, it keeps us from doing the things we want to do. If we are Christians, we want to do right, but there is a constant battle pushing us to do the wrong thing. We will talk more later about what we can do about this.

Let's end today by asking God to show you the desires that lead you into trouble. List some below and pray and ask God to help you overcome these things.

❖ _____   ❖ _____

❖ _____   ❖ _____

❖ _____   ❖ _____

❖ _____   ❖ _____

DAY 3: SATAN

Satan is probably the first enemy you thought of when we started learning about this, wasn't he? While Satan does have an impact on the other two enemies (the world and our flesh), we want to talk about him specifically in today's lesson.

Read 1 Peter 5:8. Who is the verse talking about?

_____

_____

How does the Bible describe what Satan is trying to do?

Let's read about someone in the Bible who was attacked by Satan. Turn to Matthew 4:1. Who was tempted by the devil? _____

Jesus was tempted three times in the desert. Before we look at exactly how Satan attacked and tried to "devour" Him, read verse 2 and write the particular conditions that Jesus was facing before Satan arrived on the scene.

_____

The Bible says Jesus hadn't eaten in 40 days. He was more than just a little hungry, wasn't He?! When I'm hungry it's hard to think straight, much less fight off the enemy. But Jesus did it perfectly.

Read Matthew 4:3-11 and fill in the chart below.

VERSES	TEMPTATION	JESUS' RESPONSE

We are going to talk more tomorrow about how Jesus fought the devil and how we can do it, too. But there is one thing I want to make sure you notice about this account. Read verse 11 again. After Jesus resisted the devil three times, what did the devil do?

_____

James 4:7 tells us if we resist the devil, he will flee from us. Isn't this great news? We can beat him! I can't wait to show you some really practical ways the Bible gives us to beat the devil. What we learned about Jesus today will help us as we study.

Let's turn back to 1 Peter 5:8 again before we end today. The first few words of the verse tell us what we need to do about this prowling lion who is waiting to devour us. What does it say?

_____

_____

We must remember to be watchful and alert, ready for anything Satan throws our way. Stop right now and pray and ask God to help you do that.

DAY 4:

WHAT ARE WE GOING TO DO ABOUT IT?

So far this week we've talked about three enemies that are trying to keep us from obeying God. List them below.

#1_____

#2_____

#3_____

Now let's dig into the Bible to see what we need to do about these enemies. Turn to Ephesians 6:10-13. Read it out loud very slowly to make sure you get each part clearly.

Name three ways we can withstand the schemes (wiles) of the devil.

BE STRONG IN _____ (v. 10)

PUT ON _____ (v. 11)

STAND _____ (v. 13 ESV)

Most people read these verses without ever looking at where they are found in

the Bible. But did you notice? Look up at the beginning of chapter 6 in Ephesians. What do the first few verses talk about?

_____

Verses 5-9 go on and talk about obeying who?_____

So that means so far in Ephesians, we've been commanded to obey our parents, teachers, and leaders. Have you ever struggled to do that? I know I sure have. I'm thankful verse 10 starts off talking about HOW we choose to beat Satan and actually obey God.

How do you think we can be strong in the Lord and beat Satan? What do you think that means we will need to do? Write some of your ideas down. Tomorrow we are going to see what the Bible says about it.

_____

_____

_____

_____

With such strong enemies it might sometimes feel like we have no chance of getting this right. But that's not true. Remember what we learned in week 1. When Jesus died on the cross we were freed from the POWER of sin. That means we can choose to do right.

Write your name on the line below and then these words after it "can choose to do right."

_____

Now say it out loud three times and then stop and ask God to help you believe it!

DAY 5:

THE ARMOR OF GOD

Today we are going to see six things God has given to help us in the battle against our enemies. Paul calls it the armor of God. Look up the definition of armor in the dictionary and tell why you think Paul uses this word.

_____

_____

_____

Now let's take a look at the six pieces of armor. Quickly read through Ephesians 6:14-20 and label the soldier.

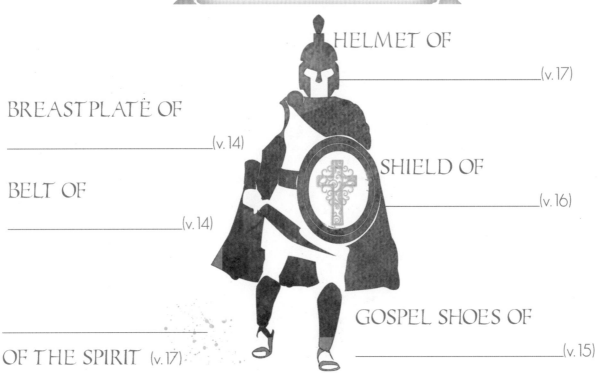

THE ARMOR OF GOD

HELMET OF

_____ (v. 17)

BREASTPLATE OF

_____ (v. 14)

BELT OF

_____ (v. 14)

SHIELD OF

_____ (v. 16)

_____

OF THE SPIRIT (v. 17)

GOSPEL SHOES OF

_____ (v. 15)

What is the first piece of armor mentioned? _____

Today we will see that each piece is important if we are going to fight against temptation and the devil. But this first piece is the foundation for it all. Without truth, we can't possibly win. Just like your belt keeps your pants from falling down, truth keeps Christians from falling down. Look up John 17:17 and write it below.

_____

_____

Each piece of armor is a gift from God.. We cannot be righteous on our own. But God gives us righteousness to protect us from evil. Notice that the breastplate is worn over your heart. Read Proverbs 4:23 and write why we need to protect our heart.

_____

In our house we put on shoes when we are ready to go somewhere. God gives us the gospel shoes of peace so we can be ready to share His Word with others and to flee from things that will harm us. What would you share with a friend in trouble?

_____

_____

A shield is used to deflect what? (see v. 16) _____

Notice the beginning of verse 16 tells us that we will need our shield of faith in all circumstances. This is how we can fight in those moments when life is really hard.

A helmet protects you from death in a battle since injury to your head is usually fatal. Salvation also saves us from death, as we are given eternal life through Jesus. Do you wear your helmet of salvation? If so, write your testimony below.

_____

_____

_____

The final piece of armor is the sword of the Spirit, which is what? _____(v. 17)

Of course, if the Word of God is our sword we are going to need to know what it says, aren't we? It won't do us any good to have our sword sitting on the shelf collecting dust. When temptation comes our way, we won't be able to find it to help us!

Read Matthew 4:4. This is one of the verses that Jesus used to fight Satan in the wilderness. Finish it below.

MAN DOES NOT LIVE BY BREAD ALONE,
BUT BY_____

End today by praying and asking God to help you read and memorize His Word and prepare your heart for battle against your enemies by putting on each piece of armor each day!

DAY 1: NO EXCUSES

This week we are going to look at five different people in the Bible who sinned against God. Each story is included in the Bible to teach us, so let's see what we can learn.

Read 1 Samuel 15:1-3. What did God tell King Saul to do and what specifically did God tell him NOT to do?

_____

_____

_____

Now read 1 Samuel 15:7-9. Did King Saul obey God's commands? (Look closely for one word that tells you WHO spared the things.)

_____

_____

_____

Of course, God is very angry over what Saul did and in verse 10 He tells Samuel that He regrets ever making Saul the king. Ouch! That's definitely not what I would want God to say about me if He had trusted a big job to me like He did Saul.

When Samuel questions Saul about his choices, he acts like he did everything right. Read 1 Samuel 15:13. Have you ever done something wrong, but then tried to pretend like everything was ok because you were hoping no one would notice?

_____

_____

_____

Saul makes matters worse by telling Samuel that they spared the best things so they could offer a sacrifice to God, but Samuel gets impatient with him. It seems then that Saul starts to really understand he's in big trouble, so he changes the story. Read verses 20-21. What is he claiming now?

_____

_____

Read 1 Samuel 15:22. Fill in the blank

TO OBEY IS BETTER THAN _____.

Saul learns two valuable lessons here. First, obeying God is better than offering Him worship or sacrifice. God always wants us to obey Him first. Not to take matters into our own hands and decide what we think might be best. He also learns something else.

Read 1 Samuel 15:24. Why does Saul say he disobeyed God?

_____

_____

_____

To be honest, it's hard to know why Saul disobeyed God because he offered up so many excuses. But this last excuse is one we are all guilty of. Write about a time when you disobeyed God because you were afraid of people (either afraid of something they would do or something they would think.)

_____

_____

_____

_____

_____

_____

_____

_____

This story is a very sad one as the Lord was never again with Saul. Although he remained king for many years after that, there was nothing but trouble in his kingdom and his heart. Take some time and pray, asking Him to help you obey fully and not be afraid of what people think or say.

DAY 2:
TAKE RESPONSIBILITY FOR YOUR ACTIONS

Today we are going to read a very familiar story. Turn to Genesis 3. I'm sure you've read this story before. Write a summary of what happened below.

_____

_____

_____

_____

_____

_____

As you know, Satan tricked Eve into eating the forbidden fruit. There are so many things we can learn from this story, but we are going to focus on what happened after the sin was committed. Read verses 8-13. Fill in the diagram by drawing arrows from the person to the person they blamed.

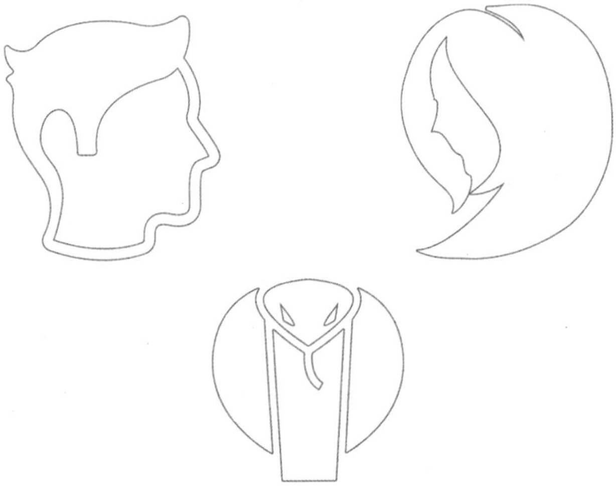

When God asked Adam and Eve why they disobeyed Him, everyone started pointing fingers at someone else. Instead of admitting what they did, they blamed each other.

Have you ever done something like this? What happened?

_____

_____

_____

_____

_____

_____

Adam and Eve tried to hide their sin from God and then they tried to blame each other instead of admitting what they did wrong. Read the following verses and write what the Bible says about this.

PSALM 32:3-4 _____

_____

NUMBERS 32:23 _____

_____

Read Proverbs 28:13 and write it below.

_____

What happens when we conceal (or hide) our sins? _____

What happens when we confess our sins? _____

God is faithful to forgive us if we ask instead of blaming others or making excuses for what we did wrong. Take time right now and ask God to forgive you for blaming others or making excuses when you disobey. Be sure to ask for forgiveness for the time you mentioned above if you haven't already.

_____
_____
_____
_____

_____
_____
_____
_____
_____
_____

DAY 3:

YOUR CHOICES AFFECT OTHERS

Today we are going to look at another story where someone hid their sins. Turn to Joshua 6. In this story the Israelites were finally living in the promised land. They took the city of Jericho with the famous battle scene most of us know (walking around the city seven times and then shouting). Read Joshua 6:18. What very specific instructions did God give them about this battle and what warning did He give if they disobeyed?

_____

_____

_____

_____

_____

_____

Chapter 7 opens up with bad news for everyone. Read verse 1 and write the name of the man who caused trouble and what he did.

_____

The end of verse 1 tells us that the anger of the Lord burned against Israel. Did you catch that? Hardly seems fair that the whole nation was in trouble because of one guy, but that was the case. Read Joshua 7:2-5 and write what happened because of Achan's sin.

_____

_____

_____

What was their punishment? (v. 24-26)

_____

_____

_____

Can you even imagine? Achan's entire family and even all of his animals were killed because he stole the devoted things from Jericho. His sins affected his family, the entire nation of Israel, and himself.

We often think that our wrong choices won't have an effect on anyone else, but this story makes it clear that's not true. And it makes sense. Think about Cain and Abel. When Cain killed Abel, his sin affected Abel (who was now dead), his parents, Cain, AND all of Cain's future family. Sin is like that. It affects so much more than us.

Today it's very unlikely you will be stoned because of the sins of someone in your family. However, since we are in relationships with other people, we will also feel the effects of their sins. Just like Cain and Abel's family. Can you think of a time when you did something that caused trouble for others? Write about it below and write out a prayer asking God to forgive you. If you can't think of anything, write a prayer asking God to help you see how your behavior hurts other people around you.

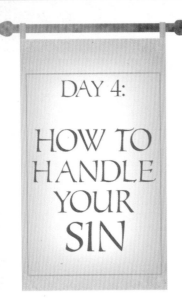

DAY 4:

HOW TO HANDLE YOUR SIN

So far this week we've seen three examples of what NOT to do when we fail and sin against God. Now let's look at some examples of what we should do!

Do you remember a few days ago when King Saul disobeyed God? As a consequence for his actions, God anointed a new king. Read Acts 13:22 and write what God had to say about this new king.

_____

_____

_____

Wouldn't you love for God to say such wonderful words about you? I know I would! God trusted David to obey, and for the most part he did. But no one is perfect. In fact, 2 Samuel 11-12 records one time when King David really blew it. David took another man's wife and had him killed to cover it all up. It was a terrible thing to do and although God still loved David, He punished him severely for his behavior. God sent the prophet Nathan in to help David see his sin.

Once David realized what he had done, his response was perfect. Read 2 Samuel 12:13. Did he make any excuses?

_____

Psalm 51 was written by David in response to how he felt about this sinful act. Many people today use parts of this Psalm to pray and ask God to forgive their sins. In fact, several verses are probably familiar to you. Read the whole chapter and write below the phrases you would like to pray when you've disobeyed God.

❖ _____   ❖ _____

❖ _____   ❖ _____

❖ _____   ❖ _____

❖ _____   ❖ _____

David shows us that confession and repentance are the most important steps to take if we've disobeyed God. Do you know what those words mean? Look them up in a Bible dictionary and write the meaning below.

CONFESSION _____

REPENTANCE _____

Another Psalm David wrote about repentance is Psalm 32. Read verses 3-5. Illustrate what happens if we hide our sins versus what happens when we confess and repent.

HIDE	CONFESS

It's important to know that repentance is much more than being sorry. True repentance is turning to the Lord and AWAY from sin. Read Acts 3:19 and write the verse below. (If you are using ESV write verse 20 as well.)

_____

_____

_____

_____

Now go back and underline the two benefits we gain from repenting. You should find a phrase that tells us our sins will be blotted out or wiped away. The second one is my favorite. When we repent and turn to God, we will have times of refreshing from the presence of the Lord. Once we've asked for forgiveness, it's God's presence with us that will restore us and heal our hearts.

Before we end today, be sure to pray and ask God to forgive you for anything you haven't confessed and repented of. Then pray the words of Psalm 51:10-12. Just read them out loud and ask God to make this your heart's cry.

DAY 5:

COME BACK WITH A CONTRITE HEART

Let's read another story of someone who is a good example to us. Read Luke 15: 11-13. Tell who this story is about and what he did wrong. Be sure to look up the words in verse 13 that you don't know so you can fully understand what he did.

_____

_____

_____

_____

_____

Draw a picture showing how bad things really got for the prodigal son after reading verses 14-16.

Once he realized how much he had messed up, he came up with a plan. Read verses 17-19 and write about this plan below.

_____

_____

Finally, let's see what his father did in verses 20-24. Are you surprised by the father's reaction? If so, tell why.

_____

_____

_____

Whenever we do the wrong thing, it's easy to believe that we can never make it right again. We might be afraid that no one will believe us or forgive us. We might even believe that we can't trust ourselves to fix things. But all of this is such a lie. This is what the enemy wants us to believe about ourselves. The story of the prodigal son is here to remind us that God will ALWAYS forgive us. All we need to do is come back.

Read 1 John 1:9 and write it below.

_____

_____

_____

The Bible promises that if we confess our sins, God is faithful to forgive. Not sometimes. EVERY single time! But there is one thing I really want you to notice about this story. Look back at verses 18-19. What kind of attitude did the prodigal son have?

Do you see where he admitted his sins and humbly asked his father to allow him to come back? He didn't even ask to be considered his son again, only to be hired as a servant. We can't miss this important point. True repentance involves a humble heart and a willingness to do anything to make it right.

Let's go back and read another part of Psalm 51 from yesterday. Look closely at verses 16-17. What kind of heart does God desire?

_____ AND _____

CONTRITE MEANS "REPENTANT AND SORROWFUL"

God doesn't want our sacrifices. He wants our hearts to be broken, repentant, and sorrowful over our sins. What do you think this looks like? Think about a time when you did the wrong thing and how you responded. Was it broken and contrite? What could you have done differently? End today with a prayer asking God to help you come back to Him with the right attitude.

_____

_____

_____

_____

_____

DAY 1:

DID GOD REALLY SAY?

So far in this study we've covered a lot about sin and doing right. This week we are going to look at four questions people often ask about this topic. You've probably asked these questions too, so pay close attention to what God wants to teach you this week.

Let's start by looking back at Genesis 3. We already know that Satan is our enemy and that he wants to keep us from obeying God. Let's read Genesis 3:1 again. Write down the first four words Satan says to Eve.

_____

Those first four words are a question. Depending on the translation you are reading you might find, "Did God really say?" Or "Did God actually say?" Satan's very first attack on people was to convince us that God probably didn't REALLY say what we've been taught He said. Have you ever thought about this question?

In today's culture it's the number one excuse people are using to make choices that go against God's Word. Did God REALLY say we can't do this or that? Take a minute and talk with your parents about some things that society is questioning about God. Write one word for each of them in the box below

Let's look up a few verses about Satan. After reading 2 Corinthians 11:14 and John 8:44, write words that describe his character on the lines below.

❖ _____   ❖ _____

❖ _____   ❖ _____

❖ _____   ❖ _____

❖ _____   ❖ _____

Now look back at the armor of God we studied. Which piece of armor do you need to find the lies of the devil? (Hint: think about the weapon that Jesus used in the wilderness.)

_____

If we are going to stand firm in the Lord and withstand the temptations of the devil, we will need the sword of the Spirit, which is the Word of God. We need to read it, know it, and memorize it. Tell why we need to do all three in the space below. Then pray and ask God to help you be ready to fight the enemy and not doubt the things God has said in His Word.

_____

_____

_____

_____

I have one final thought for you today. Read 2 Corinthians 11:3. Paul is telling the people in Corinth that he fears they are being led astray by the tricks Satan is playing on their minds. What kind of devotion to Christ does he tell them they should have? (KJV only has one word, ESV has two.)

_____AND_____

This is a very important truth for us to remember today. Satan wants confusion in our hearts. God desires a simple and pure faith. Let's be careful not to get tangled up in confusion!

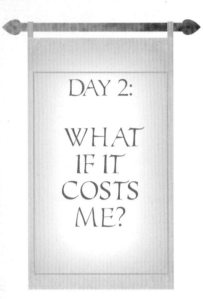

DAY 2:

WHAT IF IT COSTS ME?

If you truly want to serve Christ and live your life for Him, you want to do the right thing. As we've already learned, that doesn't mean you always will do the right thing, but the desire is always there. Many things keep us from doing what we want to do. List some of the things we've already talked about below.

_____

_____

Another thing that keeps people from doing right is the cost. Often, making the choice to do right costs us something. It might be that we have to give up our desires or wants. Or it might be that doing the right thing could cost us a friend. Or even our lives.

There were many people in the Bible who made the right decision despite the chance of losing friends or facing death. I think of David who fought Goliath, Daniel who slept with lions because he continued to pray to God even when the law said not to, and Noah who built an ark while all of his friends were laughing at him.

What do you think these men felt when they made the right choice? Do you think it was super easy at first? How do you think they felt when it was all over?

_____

_____

_____

Good friends should be there to help you walk humbly with the Lord. They should support you, encourage you, and lead you to do things that are right. The trouble is, even good Christians sin. (We've already learned that, haven't we?) This means your friends are going to make mistakes, too.

This is what happened to Job. If you've never read his story, he's the guy who lost everything in one day: his house, his children, all of his animals, and even his health. You could say it was the worst day ever and you wouldn't be exaggerating. But even though it was a very difficult day, Job did not hate God. In fact, he praised Him.

The saddest part of the story is the response of Job's wife and friends. Read Job 2:9. What does Job's wife tell him to do?

_____

_____

Now read verse 10. How does Job respond?

_____

Many chapters in the book of Job are devoted to the speeches that his three friends gave him. They weren't supportive, friendly, or helpful. In fact, they were very much hurtful. Can you think of a time in your life when things weren't going well and your friend (or family member) did something to make it worse?

_____

_____

It would be easy to let friends lead us astray when life is tough, but the Bible gives us different advice.

Read Psalm 1:1
There are three kinds of people mentioned in this verse.
List them.

This verse tells us not to walk with, stand with, or sit with these people, but to get our counsel from what? (See verse 2.)

_____

If you have a friend who keeps asking you to do the wrong thing, what will you do about it this week? (Hint: if you are not sure, ask your parents to help you.) Write a commitment to God about this problem in the space below.

_____

_____

_____

_____

_____

_____

DAY 3:

BUT NO ONE WILL KNOW, RIGHT?

When I was younger I had many friends who were bad influences like Job's friends AND who were tricky like Satan. One of the things they always said was, "No one will ever know." Maybe your friends have said this, too. Or maybe you say it to yourself.

It's ok to eat this cookie, because no one will ever know.

It's ok to go somewhere we are not allowed to go, because no one will ever know.

It's ok to steal this toy from the store, because no one will ever know.

Draw or write about a time when you thought no one would know. What happened?

This lie has been around since the beginning of time. In fact, Adam and Eve hid from God when they sinned. I don't think they believed He wouldn't know, but I'm sure they were hoping that! Just like Adam and Eve, we like to hide our sin. We try to make sure we look good on the outside, but don't worry as much about the stuff no one sees.

Is this the right thing to do? Let's see what the Bible says. Read Luke 12:2. What does this verse say about hidden things?

_____

What does Proverbs 15:3 say? Write it below.

_____

_____

_____

The Bible is clear that God knows every single time we sin. Nothing is hidden from Him. Read Psalm 139:2. What else does God know about us?

_____

It's very tempting to do the right thing when people are looking and then do our own thing when we think no one is looking. But we must remember that doing right is not a show. In fact, it's what we do when no one is looking that really shows who we are.

There is no chance of tricking God by looking good on the outside. Read 1 Samuel 16:7. What does the Lord look at? In the heart below, write some things you want the Lord to see when He looks at your heart. Pray and ask Him to help you do right.

DAY 4: WHY BOTHER?

Today we are going to talk about a question that is very hard for some people to understand. If Jesus died for our sins and always forgives us, why shouldn't we just keep on sinning?

This is a question most adults have a hard time answering because it seems so confusing. Is it true that Jesus will forgive us for an unlimited amount of sins? Yes, it is. But trust me when I tell you that we DON'T want to just keep doing it. Let's dig into the Bible and see why.

Read Numbers 32:23 and fill in the blank.

BE SURE _____

Most people think this means that God will always know your sins. That's true. But this verse really means much more than that. It means our sins will follow us around forever. They have consequences. Even forgiven sins have consequences.

Remember King Saul? King David? Both of these men repented of their sin. Both faced serious consequences. Do you remember what they were? King Saul was removed as king and lost the favor of the Lord. King David lost his baby and faced great tragedy in his family for decades after repenting. Sin is no joke. Read Galatians 6:7-8.

Draw what this verse means.

The Bible makes it clear that we may face serious consequences for our sin, but this isn't the only reason to avoid it. Let's read Romans 1:21. What happens to the heart of a person who doesn't honor God?

_____

The more we sin, the harder it gets to become free from the power of that sin. Just like we talked about in Week 1, sin makes us a slave and we can't break free. Even Christians can live as slaves if we refuse to repent and walk away from sin. And before long, our hearts can get so dark, we don't hear God calling us back to safety.

Read Ephesians 4:18-19. What happens to us when our hearts are darkened?

_____

_____

_____

As you can see, the choice to keep on sinning is a very bad one. We don't want God to give us over to our desires so we will forever be slaves to them. We don't want to face the consequence of this kind of sin either. End today by praying and asking God to help you never believe this lie.

_____

_____

_____

_____

_____

_____

_____

_____

_____

_____

DAY 5:
THE BATTLE PLAN

We've learned so much in this past month about doing right. I hope you've had fun and that you've listened to what God was teaching you. Before we finish this study, let's take a few minutes and review what we've learned.

Let's be ready to go out and fight! What are your three enemies? Draw them below.

What are six tools God has given you for fighting these enemies and making RIGHT choices?

THE ARMOR OF GOD

_____ (v. 14)

_____ (v. 17)

(v. 14)

_____ (v. 16)

_____ (v. 17)

_____ (v. 17)

I pray that you are ready to do whatever it takes to fight the battle against evil and win at doing right as much as you possibly can. Remember, doing right is just one step at a time. It's one right choice and then another and then another. God isn't asking you to be perfect. This journey on earth is all about preparing us to be with Him. It's a process.

Let's finish this study by reading one last verse: James 1:12. Once we have stood the tests and trials God puts in our path, what will we get? Draw it in the box.. Take some time and really make it look as amazing as the words describe it.

Isn't that a beautiful promise? It's true that we will need to put on our armor and fight against our enemies in this life, but God promises that one day we will receive a wonderful prize for it. It won't be at all like anything we could ever imagine, but we know it will be worth the fight!

Before you close this book write a testimony telling all that God has taught you in this study. If you feel led to do so, write some commitments that you made throughout the study to work harder or grow closer to the image of Christ.

_____

_____

_____

_____

_____

_____

_____

_____

_____

_____

_____

_____

_____

_____